Recognizing Inflation in Accounting

by Francis J. Walsh, Jr.
Director, Special Financial Projects

A Research Report from The Conference Board

Contents

Exhibit

Foreword

ONE OF THE OBJECTIVES of The Conference Board's research program is to help improve the level of public understanding of financial accounting and auditing. The Board hopes that such heightened public awareness will lead to better financial reporting and disclosure by business enterprises and by other economic entities.

This report is one of the instruments through which The Conference Board seeks to achieve its objective. It is a concise summary of what has been accomplished so far in the long-running attempt to remove the distortive effects of inflation from the financial reports of business enterprises. These attempts and experiments can be described in general terms as "inflation accounting."

Although there is an abundance of technical accounting literature on the problem of inflation and how to deal with it in the financial reports of business enterprises, most of it is directed to accounting practitioners and their interests. The Conference Board believes that general readers also need an overview of this important but difficult subject.

Such understanding is needed especially at this time by readers of corporate annual reports containing the newly mandated disclosures of inflationary effects. Although these requirements apply at present only to large corporations, a continuation of high rates of inflation is likely to spur demands for much more widespread applications of inflation accounting. The Conference Board hopes that this publication will help to answer the questions of business executives, investors and students who are confronted for the first time by inflation adjustments.

This report is a product of the Special Financial Projects Department, a section of the Management Research Division, Harold Stieglitz, Vice President.

KENNETH A. RANDALL
President

Chapter 1
Introduction

LEARNING TO LIVE WITH INFLATION is a painful experience. Most adult Americans grew up in a world in which prices were comparatively stable for long periods of time and a "sound dollar" was taken for granted. The deepening erosion in purchasing power of the dollar in recent years, however, has shaken the confidence of vast numbers of people in the ability of the U.S. dollar to continue to perform the basic monetary functions of serving as a reliable unit of measurement and as a storehouse of value. As a result, people and organizations are altering the conduct of their economic affairs to try to cope with rising prices. Incurrence of heavy burdens of debt, speculation in items that are regarded as hedges against inflation—for example, antiques and works of art—and the rush to buy real estate are only a few indications of general recognition of the inroads of inflation.

One area where the idea of adapting to the reality of inflation has met with rather stiff resistance, however, is financial accounting. Not that the issue of recognizing inflation in financial statements of business enterprises has been neglected—far from it. The questions of whether and how to present inflation-adjusted financial data are among the most intensively studied and debated topics in the history of accounting. But, until recently, most businesspeople and accountants who had to wrestle with the practical, day-to-day problems of the marketplace seemed to regard inflation accounting principally as an academic curiosity. Perhaps accountants felt that inflation adjustments, with all their technical complexities, would quietly drop out of sight when prices returned to normal. And, few businesspeople could be expected to support an accounting refinement that usually results in lower reported earnings.

Such attitudes prevailed as long as inflation remained relatively mild in this country. But the problem could hardly be ignored when inflation rates soared to the double-digit level. Accordingly, both the Securities and Exchange Commission and the Financial Accounting Standards Board acted to compel large corporations, at least, to take account of the impact of inflation in their financial disclosures to the public.

Perhaps, if the forces of inflation should weaken, the pressures for inflation-adjusted financial data would also ease. Few, if any, economic forecasters, however, predict much permanent relief from rising prices. Consequently, it is reasonable to expect that inflation-accounting techniques will gradually be applied to ever-increasing numbers of business enterprises.

Chapter 2
The Problem of Inflation
in Accounting

ONE OF THE UNDERLYING CONVENTIONS of accounting requires that the data entering into the financial reporting process be expressed in terms of money. Furthermore, in observance of the principle of historical cost, transactions are permanently recorded in the number of units of money actually flowing into or out of the enterprise at the time each transaction occurred. This rule is followed regardless of the changes that may take place in the purchasing power of money over time. Conventional accounting, in other words, does not recognize the differences in purchasing power between dollars currently being circulated and those that changed hands in the past.

Thus, for example, an asset purchased twenty years ago, another bought five years ago, and a third acquired earlier this year, are aggregated in the balance sheet of the enterprise in terms of the number of dollars expended to buy these assets at the time they were acquired. The purchasing powers of each "package" of dollars however, are obviously different from each other, and they are probably different from what the same number of dollars would buy today. The number of dollars presently needed to *replace* the older items would likewise differ considerably from their original purchase prices.

Differences in the purchasing power of money also affect the income statement. As items in the corporate balance sheet are used up in generating revenue, their monetary values are transferred to the income statement in the process of matching revenues and costs. This process is most easily observed in the case of plant and equipment items—the expired portion of their costs are reflected periodically in the income statement as depreciation expense. It is apparent that the revenues and costs that are matched in the income statement are expressed in terms of different groupings of dollars that have widely different purchasing powers. Under the rules of conventional accounting, these differences in the purchasing power of different blocks of money are not recognized. Every set of conventionally prepared financial statements, therefore, contains a conglomeration of dollars: some having present-day purchasing power, and others expressing the purchasing powers of various times in the past.

In addition to the distortions created by aggregating dollars of varying purchasing power, inflation also has another economic effect that is not recognized in conventional financial reporting. It is well known that holders of items such as cash and receivables suffer a real economic loss during a time of inflation because the purchasing power of such assets diminishes simply with the passage of time. Conversely, a debtor whose obligations are denominated in a fixed number of dollars enjoys a gain because the debts will be repaid with dollars of less purchasing power than the ones received when the debt was incurred. These economic effects are known as "holding gains and losses" and they are not measured and reported in the usual historical-dollar financial statements.

The distortive effects of inflation on the conventionally prepared financial statements of business enterprises are, of course, quite familiar to accountants and to well-informed

4

consumers of financial information. For at least the past three decades, some accounting practitioners and researchers have been studying and calling attention to the misleading information contained in many financial reports during a time of inflation. And, business executives in capital-intensive industries have been alarmed at the erosion of capital that takes place when depreciation expense is computed on the basis of historical costs in the company's income tax returns. Until recently, however, there has been very little general interest in any of the proposed remedies. Probably the main reason why the inflation problem in accounting has been ignored for so long is that the rate of inflation, for many years, was simply not considered severe enough to warrant the extra cost and complexity that inflation accounting would require. However, in recent years, inflation has been so severe, so persistent, and apparently so entrenched in the economy, that there has been growing pressure for disclosure of inflation's effects on corporate financial statements.

1980

Responding to this perceived demand, both the Securities and Exchange Commission (SEC) and the Financial Accounting Standards Board (FASB) have decreed that certain business enterprises must inform investors of the effects of rising prices on the financial statements of these reporting companies. The SEC's requirements were stated in its Accounting Series Release (ASR) No. 190, issued in 1976. In November, 1979, the Commission announced that it had repealed the provisions of ASR No. 190 once the requirements of the FASB became fully effective. These FASB rules were set forth in the Board's Statement No. 33, "Financial Reporting and Changing Prices," which was released in October, 1979.

Even though both of these official pronouncements (see box on p. 6) are attempts to deal with the same problem of changing prices, the approaches of the two regulatory bodies were quite different and the quantitative results of applying each agency's rules to the same set of financial statements

The SEC and the FASB

The Securities and Exchange Commission (SEC) is the government agency charged with enforcing the federal securities laws. Since the 1930's, this agency has had the statutory power to make and enforce accounting rules for corporations that come under its jurisdiction. The SEC, however, has traditionally delegated to private-sector agencies the task of developing financial accounting standards. For many years, this task was carried out by the Committee on Accounting Procedure, and later by the Accounting Principles Board—both units of the American Institute of Certified Public Accountants.

In 1973, the Financial Accounting Standards Board, a new, independent institution (still in the private sector) took over the duty of financial accounting rule making. The SEC formally declared its support of the FASB in its Accounting Series Release No. 150, and, in effect, any corporation that fails to observe FASB pronouncements in its financial reports violates SEC regulations.

would not be likely to agree. One of the objectives of this publication is to explain why such discrepancies exist.

At the time of writing this report, the disclosures mandated by the Securities and Exchange Commission and by the Financial Accounting Standards Board applied only to a comparatively small number of large corporations. But, if the strong inflationary forces in the nation's economy continue unabated, it is likely that inflation adjustments will appear eventually in the financial reports of a much greater number of enterprises. Thus, consumers of financial information will be confronted by inflation accounting with increasing frequency.

In spite of the fact that inflation adjustments and methods of reporting them have been studied for many years, there is no general agreement as to how this information should be presented to investors, nor any widely accepted format for

6

doing so. Recognizing the unsettled nature of this aspect of financial reporting, both the FASB and the SEC have gone on record as favoring experimentation and innovation by the preparers of financial statements. And the FASB has emphasized that its recommendations in Statement No. 33 should be viewed as guidelines, rather than as firmly settled solutions to the problems of inflation accounting. There is, therefore, much to be learned about inflation accounting through practical experience. Corporate managements, as well as their outside auditors, will have a strong influence on the development of methods and techniques of presenting inflation adjustments as experience is gained with this new development in financial reporting.

Chapter 3
Approaches to Inflation Accounting

EVEN ASSUMING GENERAL AGREEMENT on the need to remove the distortive effects of inflation from financial statements, there is no unanimity of opinion among accountants as to how best to do it. Basically, there are two approaches to the calculation of inflation adjustments. Not only do they differ in their theoretical bases, but they also produce different results when applied to the same set of historical-cost financial records. For the sake of uniformity in terminology, the names of these approaches, as defined by the Financial Accounting Standards Board, will be used in this report, although both have been described in accounting literature over the years by various other labels. These two approaches to inflation accounting are (1) constant-dollar accounting, and (2) current-cost accounting.

Applying the techniques of either one of these two approaches to conventional, historical-cost financial statements results in a set of restated financial reports which can then be compared with the basic, conventional statements to measure the effects of inflation on a business enterprise, especially on net income. Disclosure of these effects to investors and other interested readers of corporate reports is what inflation accounting is all about.

Constant Dollar Accounting

The authoritative pronouncement on inflation accounting at the present time is the FASB's Statement No. 33, "Financial Reporting and Changing Prices." This statement defines constant-dollar accounting as: "A method of reporting financial statement elements in dollars each of which has the same (i.e., constant) general purchasing power. This method of accounting is often described as accounting in units of general purchasing power or as accounting in units of current purchasing power."[1]

The important element in this definition for the purposes of this discussion is the concept of reporting in dollars of the same *general* purchasing power. Constant-dollar accounting differs fundamentally from the current cost accounting approach in this emphasis on changes in general purchasing power, rather than on changes in prices of specific commodities or groups of commodities.

Techniques of Constant Dollar Accounting

Basically, the constant-dollar approach takes the amounts of historical dollars contained in the financial records of a business enterprise and applies a general price index to these historical dollar balances to restate them in terms of dollars of uniform purchasing power as of the date of the balance sheet. A simple example of such a restatement follows:

Assume a machine having a historical cost of $10,000 was acquired two years ago and the relevant general price-level index that year was 100. During the intervening period, the general price-level index increased 20 percent. The restated

---

[1]Statement of Financial Accounting Standards No. 33, "Financial Reporting and Changing Prices," September, 1979. Copyright © Financial Accounting Standards Board of the Financial Accounting Foundation, High Ridge Park, Stamford, Connecticut 06905.

amount to be reported for this asset on the latest balance sheet of the enterprise is $12,000, determined as follows:

Historical Cost		Index		Restated Amount
$10,000	x	120/100	=	$12,000

Restatements such as this are calculated for all items in the balance sheet that are classified as "nonmonetary," that is, those items whose realizable amounts are not fixed by some kind of contract. "Monetary" items, in contrast, are those balance-sheet items whose amounts are fixed by some kind of contractual arrangement. For example, the balance of a checking account at a bank or the balance of a receivable from a customer are fixed, contractual, monetary amounts that would not rise or fall due to changes in general purchasing power of the dollar. Nonmonetary items, however, are not fixed and may be restated in terms of changes in the general price level.

In the methodology of constant-dollar accounting, monetary items are important because they give rise to "holding gains and losses" (see Chapter 2). These holding gains and losses are calculated and their aggregate amount is reported as an item in the restated income statement under some such caption as "Holding Gain (Loss) on Monetary Items."

A set of restated constant-dollar financial statements, consequently, includes a balance sheet containing a mixed collection of monetary items that are reported in terms of their contractually realizable amounts, and nonmonetary items that have been restated in terms of the present-day general purchasing power of the historical dollars expended or acquired in connection with these items. The restated balance of retained earnings represents the net effects of these restatements.

The income restatement in a constant-dollar world contains general revenue and expense categories restated in pretty much the same ways as indicated for nonmonetary

Other Terminology

One of the confusing features of inflation accounting is that, over the years, various authors have invented different terms to describe essentially the same thing. An example of such confusion is what is now called constant-dollar accounting. For a long time, this approach was called "price-level accounting" (or, alternatively, "price-level adjustments"). This was the terminology most frequently used by the American Institute of Certified Public Accountants and its Accounting Principles Board during their studies and recommendations of the 1960's. Essentially, however, constant-dollar accounting and price-level accounting mean the same thing: restatement of historical-dollar financial statement items into dollars of current purchasing power by means of an index of general price-level changes.

items on the balance sheet. Of course, depreciation expense and cost of goods sold are sharply higher as a result of the restated fixed assets and inventory balances on the balance sheet. And, in addition, the income statement accounts for holding gains or losses on monetary items.

The Index Number Problem

One of the points at issue in the case of constant-dollar accounting is the question of what index of general purchasing power to use for restating the historical dollar amounts. The Financial Accounting Standards Board designated the Consumer Price Index for all Urban Consumers, published by the Bureau of Labor Statistics of the U.S. Department of Labor, as the index to be used in complying with Statement No. 33. In contrast, a decade earlier, the Accounting Principles Board recommended the GNP deflator.[2] The American Institute of Certified Public

[2]Accounting Principles Board Statement No. 3, "Financial Statements Restated for General Price Level Changes," June, 1969. American Institute of Certified Public Accountants, 1211 Avenue of the Americas, New York, New York 10036.

Accountants' research study, which preceded the 1969 APB recommendation, contained a detailed treatment of the index number problem.[3] (This document is strongly recommended to readers who are deeply interested in this complex phase of inflation accounting.) There seems to be fairly general agreement that no price index is completely satisfactory for the purposes of constant-dollar accounting. But one argument in favor of the Consumer Price Index is that it is available on a monthly basis.

Pros and Cons of Constant Dollar Accounting

Arguments in favor of the constant-dollar approach to inflation accounting may be summarized this way:

(1) Constant-dollar accounting retains the historical cost principle of accounting; it simply restates the historical dollars in terms of dollars having present-day purchasing power.

(2) Constant-dollar accounting measures the distortive effects of inflation and discloses the holding gains and losses arising from monetary assets and liabilities.

The principal arguments against constant-dollar accounting are:

(1) Difficulty of finding a suitable index.

(2) Complexity and possible confusion on the part of users of financial statements.

(3) Constant-dollar accounting does not measure the impact of inflation on the specific assets (especially inventories and fixed assets) owned by individual companies.

[3] "Reporting the Financial Effects of Price-Level Changes," Accounting Research Study No. 6, by the staff of the Accounting Research Division, 1963, American Institute of Certified Public Accountants.

Current Cost Accounting

FASB Statement No. 33 defines Current Cost Accounting as: "A method of measuring and reporting assets and expenses associated with the use or sale of assets, at their current cost or lower recoverable amount at the balance sheet date or at the date of use or sale."[1]

Current-cost accounting, unlike constant-dollar accounting, makes no attempt to retain its tie to historical dollars. The philosophy of current-cost accounting, in effect, declares that the dollars expended at some point in the past have no relevance in the preparation of a present-day financial statement during an inflationary period. According to this view, the only relevant numbers are the dollars that would be expended if an asset were to be acquired on the balance sheet date. Proponents of this view believe that any other method of valuation is not economically realistic during inflation.

Furthermore, current-cost accounting regards the effects of inflation on an enterprise not in terms of changes in the *general* price level, as in the case of constant-dollar accounting. Rather, it concentrates on the price level changes of the *specific* commodities or assets in which the individual firm is concerned.

The current-cost technique requires the selection of appropriate methods of determining current costs of the items to be measured. FASB Statement No. 33 suggests internally or externally generated price indexes for the class of goods or services being measured; references to current invoice prices; vendors' price lists or other quotations or estimates; and standard manufacturing costs that reflect current costs.

Advantages and Disadvantages

The principal arguments in favor of current-cost accounting center around economic realism. Supporters of this

---

[1]See footnote No. 1, page 9.

approach to inflation accounting believe that it provides a more realistic measure of the effects of inflation on an individual company because it measures the changes in prices of the specific items with which the company is concerned. They argue that inflation does not affect all firms and all commodities equally and, therefore, it is unrealistic to compute inflation adjustments by means of general price indexes.

On the other hand, opponents of current-cost accounting argue that it undermines the objectivity and integrity of financial accounting by abandoning the historical-cost principle. An outgrowth of abandoning historical cost is the difficulty of auditing the estimates of current cost. Finally, they cite the difficulty of finding suitable indexes or other indications of current costs.

Variations of Current Cost

The concept of current-cost accounting has appeared under several labels over a period of years, most frequently as "replacement value accounting" or "replacement cost accounting." The most recent manifestation of this terminology was in the SEC's 1976 mandate that certain large companies report the replacement costs of inventories and fixed assets and the effects of these valuations on cost of sales and depreciation.[4] These limited replacement cost disclosures have been required by the SEC since 1976, but in late 1979 they were rescinded once the FASB's Statement No. 33 became fully effective.

Many businesspeople objected strongly to the SEC's replacement cost requirements on the grounds that they were unrealistic. They felt it was highly unlikely that most companies would actually replace their existing productive

---

[4]Accounting Series Release No. 190, Securities and Exchange Commission, Washington, D.C. 20549, March 23, 1976, "Notice of Adoption of Amendments to Regulation S-X Requiring Disclosure of Certain Replacement Cost Data."

facilities in kind. If they replaced them with newer technology, there was no objective way to determine what their costs would actually amount to. Others objected to the SEC requirements on the grounds of incompleteness. The Commission did not require comprehensive restatement of all financial statement items and thus there was no way to assess the impact of inflation on net income. Critics of the SEC's rule believed this to be a crucial omission.

It is important to understand the fundamental differences between the constant-dollar approach and the current-cost method of inflation accounting because the Financial Accounting Standards Board's Statement No. 33 requires disclosure of the effects of applying *both* approaches in the financial reports of affected companies.

Chapter 4

Requirements of the Financial Accounting Standards Board

Begg— m 1930's — defation

THE LONG STRUGGLE to develop an authoritative pronouncement on inflation accounting came to a climax in early October, 1979, when the Financial Accounting Standards Board released its statement "Financial Reporting and Changing Prices." The Board declared that the new standard was to take effect for fiscal years ending on or after December 25, 1979. However, permission was given to postpone compliance with one requirement (presentation of current-cost information) until reporting years ending on or after December 31, 1980.

This standard was the result of work that had gone on at the FASB almost from the time it began to operate in 1973. In 1974, the Board released an exposure draft of a standard on inflation accounting based on the constant-dollar approach. That standard was never adopted because the SEC did not favor constant-dollar accounting. The Commission preferred inflation accounting based on replacement costs and, as described elsewhere in this report, it set forth its own rules in 1976, requiring replacement-cost disclosure. In the meantime, the FASB continued to study and debate the problem. Part of this study consisted of a research project in which a number of major corporations experimented with inflation-accounting techniques.

As finally issued, FASB Statement No. 33 applies only to a relatively small number of large corporations. Only those firms with assets totaling more than $1 billion, or whose inventories and property, plant and equipment (before deducting accumulated depreciation) amount to more than $125 million, are required to make the disclosures specified by the FASB. These size limitations are somewhat comparable to those set by the SEC in 1976 for compliance with its replacement-cost reporting requirement.

Disclosures Required

An accounting standard on such a complex and controversial subject as inflation accounting might be expected to be quite lengthy. And FASB Statement No. 33 is indeed a formidable document. Nevertheless, for those who have a serious interest in the subject, there is no doubt that it is required reading. (Copies of Statement No. 33 may be ordered from the Publications Department, Financial Accounting Standards Board, High Ridge Park, Stamford, Connecticut 06905.)

A key feature of the FASB's Standard is that the required information is to be disclosed in corporate annual reports to investors in unaudited *supplementary* form. The basic financial statements (balance sheet, income statement, and statement of changes in financial position) continue to be based on the same conventional, historical-cost principle as before. Many reporting companies are expected to provide their supplementary inflation disclosures in the form of notes to the financial statements; although some other firms may prefer to highlight their disclosures by giving them greater prominence than a footnote can provide.

There are three principal elements of the required supplementary disclosures:

(1) A statement of income from continuing operations adjusted for changing prices for the current reporting year. This statement must report the major elements of the income statement (a) as given in the primary statements; (b) as adjusted for general inflation (i.e., constant dollars); and (c) as adjusted for changes in specific prices (current costs). (The FASB's suggested format for such a presentation is reproduced in the Appendix to this publication on p. 48.)

(2) A five-year comparison of selected financial data adjusted to reflect the effects of both general inflation (constant dollars) and current costs: (a) income (loss) from continuing operations, actual and per common share; (b) net assets at year-end. Also required in this comparison are such data as:

(a) Sales or other operating revenue;
(b) Cash dividends per share of common stock;
(c) Inflationary gain from outstanding debt;
(d) Difference between specific prices and the general price level;
(e) Market price per common share at year-end;
(f) The average consumer price index.

(The FASB's suggested format for this-five year comparison is also reproduced in the Appendix to this report on p. 50.)

(3) Explanation by management of the significance of these disclosures.

Sources of Additional Information

The FASB was well aware of the problems that companies would have in implementing the new standard. Accordingly, in December, 1979, it released a publication, *Illustrations of Financial Reporting and Changing Prices*. This booklet was prepared by a special task group of financial officers from major corporations and it illustrates formats which firms can use to comply with the disclosure standards of Statement No.

33. In addition to this official FASB publication, many accounting firms also have prepared guidelines and other illustrative materials to assist those of their clients affected by the new requirements.

In releasing its new inflation accounting standard, the FASB has repeatedly emphasized the tentative and experimental nature of the disclosure requirements. The Board acknowledges that there is much to be learned from the practical application of inflation-accounting techniques and it encourages experimentation and further research. It has declared its intention to monitor the experience developed through this standard, particularly with regard to the usefulness of the data, and will make such future modifications as experience dictates. Also, certain industries have special problems in connection with implementing the inflation-accounting standards. The Board has announced that, from time to time, proposals will be submitted for public comment concerning these special situations.

Chapter 5
Early Experiments With Inflation Accounting

INFLATION ACCOUNTING is a subject that has been around for a long time. The disastrous inflation that took place in Germany after the first World War prompted accountants in that country to experiment with inflation-accounting techniques. Curiously enough, in the United States, it was not rising prices but deflation during the depression of the 1930's that attracted the attention of accounting theoreticians to the instability of the dollar as a unit of measurement. For example, Professor Ralph C. Jones of Yale University wrote an article, "Financial Statements and the Uncertain Dollar," that appeared in the September, 1935 *Journal of Accountancy.* Another publication on the same subject was a book, *Stabilized Accounting,* by Dr. Henry W. Sweeney, published by Harper & Brothers in 1936.

LIFO and Accelerated Depreciation

These early inquiries into the accounting effects of purchasing power fluctuations did not result in any widespread clamor for abandonment of historical-dollar financial reports. But they probably encouraged experimentation with the last-in, first-out (LIFO) method of accounting for the flow of inventory costs and with various methods of accelerated depreciation. Inventories and fixed assets are the items in the typical corporate balance sheet that are most likely to be severely affected over time by changing price levels. Some accountants and businesspeople reasoned that, by altering the *timing* of the flow of costs of inventories and fixed assets from the balance sheet to the income statement, some current relief from changing prices could be obtained—at least insofar as reporting income was concerned.

The effect of LIFO is that the cost of the most recent purchases of inventory is reflected immediately in the "cost of goods sold" section of the income statement. Therefore, in a period of rising inventory prices, current inventory purchase costs are matched against current selling prices for the company's products; and thereby the effects of rising prices on net income are somewhat neutralized. Unfortunately, LIFO produces an opposite effect on the balance sheet: The inventory cost figure represents older and older purchase prices—and thus the inventory valuation becomes further removed from reality with the passage of time and with rises in prices.

Accelerated depreciation methods (e.g., double declining balance and sum-of-the-years digits) also give some relief in the case of fixed assets during periods of inflation. These methods permit much larger write-offs of the cost of productive facilities during the early years of ownership. But, as the assets get older, the opposite effect is created.

Neither LIFO nor accelerated depreciation really gets at the heart of the inflation problem, however. They simply permit changes in the timing of the write-off of inventory and fixed-asset costs to the income statement. In the long run, the total costs reflected in the income statement are not changed and the distortive effects of inflation on the balance sheet are not helped at all. LIFO and accelerated depreciation are approved for income tax purposes and are widely used by U.S. business enterprises in their reports to shareholders as well as in their income tax returns.

Depreciation in Excess of Historical Costs

A much more direct attack on the problem of inflation was the short-lived attempt by some U.S. corporations, during the period of severe inflation after World War II, to report depreciation in excess of historical costs. The justification for these higher depreciation charges was that, in inflationary times, capital-intensive industries face ever-increasing costs of replacing their productive facilities. In such periods, depreciation computed by conventional, historical-cost methods does not provide sufficient funds for replacement of these assets. Therefore, to the extent of the shortfall, true depreciation expense is understated and net income is overstated. Finally, if dividends are declared out of the overstated earnings, the board of directors is unwittingly liquidating the company.

Neither the accounting profession nor the SEC, however, would go along with attempts to report depreciation on any basis other than historical-dollar costs. The American Institute of Certified Public Accountants' Committee on Accounting Procedure was the accounting profession's authoritative rule-making agency at that time, and it came down hard against the practice of basing depreciation on high replacement costs. In December, 1947, the Committee issued Accounting Research Bulletin No. 33, "Depreciation and High Costs."

In this Bulletin, the Committee expressed the opinion that business management, in carrying out its responsibility to provide for replacement of facilities, may properly appropriate portions of a company's net income or retained earnings to provide for high-priced replacements. But it should not attempt to accomplish this result by tampering with traditional methods of computing depreciation. The Bulletin goes on to say:

"Accounting and financial reporting for general use will best serve their purposes by adhering to the generally accepted concept of depreciation based on cost, at least until the dollar is stabilized at some level. An attempt to recognize current prices in providing depreciation, to be consistent, would require the serious step of formally recording appraised current values for all properties, and continuous and consistent depreciation charges based on the new values. Without such formal steps, there would be no objective standard by which to judge the propriety of the amounts of depreciation charges against current income, and the significance of recorded amounts of profit might be seriously impaired.

"It would not increase the usefulness of reported corporate income figures if some companies charged depreciation on appraised values while others adhered to cost. The committee believes, therefore, that consideration of radical changes in accepted accounting procedures should not be undertaken, at least until a stable price level would make it practicable for business as a whole to make the change at the same time."[1]

Less than a year later, in October, 1948, the Committee on Accounting Procedure issued a letter to the membership of the American Institute of Certified Public Accountants reaffirming the opinion stated in Accounting Research Bulletin No. 33. The Committee's conclusion was:

"Should inflation proceed so far that original dollar costs lose their practical significance, it might become necessary to restate all assets in terms of the depreciated currency, as has been done in some countries. But it does not seem to the committee that such action should be recommended now if financial statements are to have maximum usefulness to the greatest number of users."[2]

[1]American Institute of Certified Public Accountants, Accounting Research Bulletin No. 33, New York, December, 1947. The contents of this Bulletin were carried over, in June, 1953, to Accounting Research Bulletin No. 43, which is a restatement and revision of the first 42 bulletins issued by the Committee on Accounting Procedure of the American Institute of Certified Public Accountants.

[2]Letter to the membership of the American Institute of Certified Public Accountants from the Institute's Committee on Accounting Procedure, October 14, 1948.

Furthermore, the Committee reemphasized in that letter its belief that retention of earnings was the proper means by which companies might cope with inflated costs of replacing fixed assets. It went on to say:

"Stockholders, employees, and the general public should be informed that a business must be able to retain out of profits amounts sufficient to replace productive facilities at current prices if it is to stay in business. The committee therefore gives its full support to the use of supplementary financial schedules, explanations or footnotes by which management may explain the need for retention of earnings."

Experiments of the American Accounting Association

One of the most significant early attempts to confront the problem of inflation in financial statements was launched by the American Accounting Association in 1951. This is a national organization whose members are primarily educators. It has long been one of the leaders in sponsoring research aimed at the development of new knowledge in accounting.

In August, 1951, the Association's Committee on Concepts and Standards Underlying Corporate Financial Statements issued a report, "Price Level Changes and Financial Statements." Among other things, it stated that:

"Management may properly include in periodic reports to stockholders comprehensive supplementary statements which present the effects of the fluctuation in the value of the dollar upon net income and upon financial position.

"(a) Such supplementary statements should be internally consistent; the income statement and the balance sheet should both be adjusted by the same procedures, so that the figures in such complementary statements are coordinate and have the same relative significance.

24

"(b) Such supplementary statements should be reconciled in detail with the primary statements reflecting unadjusted original dollar costs, and should be regarded as an extension or elaboration of the primary statements rather than as a departure therefrom.

"(c) Such supplementary statements should be accompanied by comments and explanations clearly setting forth the implications, uses, and limitations of the adjusted data."

The report also urged intensive research and experimentation to develop experience with methods of presenting inflation-adjusted financial statements. In keeping with this recommendation, the American Accounting Association, with the financial assistance of the Merrill Foundation for the Advancement of Financial Knowledge, conducted a study of the effects of price-level changes on the financial statements of four companies. The project was directed by Professor Ralph C. Jones of Yale University, assisted by the outside auditors of the four companies that participated in the study. The four companies and the time periods for which accounting data were adjusted were:

Armstrong Cork Company	(1941-1951)
New York Telephone Company	(1940, 1946-1952)
The Reece Corporation	(1940-1951)
Sargent & Company	(1929-1952)

The project was completed and a report, "Price Level Changes and Financial Statements—Case Studies of Four Companies," written by Professor Jones in 1955. It was published by the American Accounting Association.

The purposes of the project were to:

(a) Test techniques for expressing financial statements in dollars of uniform purchasing power, using a general price index;

(b) Compare these adjusted statements with conventional financial reports in order to measure the impact of inflation on the firms;

(c) Provide managements, accountants and government bodies with some evidence of the need for and the usefulness of financial reports expressed in dollars of uniform purchasing power.

The conclusions of the report were lengthy and detailed, but they can be summarized briefly:

(1) Inflation has, indeed, impaired the usefulness of conventional accounting reports, and supplementary information disclosing these effects is needed.

(2) A measure of general purchasing power, such as the Consumer Price Index, should be used to prepare adjusted financial reports. Such adjusted reports are not a departure from the historical cost basis of accounting; they merely recognize that the dollar has changed in value.

(3) Depreciation is the financial statement item most seriously affected by inflation.

(4) Real income tax rates are raised well above statutory rates when depreciation and inventory costs are stated in historical dollars. The use of LIFO, however, mitigates this effect in the case of inventories.

(5) In the case of public utilities, it is unrealistic, in times of inflation, to base maximum allowable rates of return on earnings computed by conventional historical-cost accounting methods.

(6) The reduction of the real burden of interest expense and preferred dividend charges in times of inflation confers a real benefit on the corporation and its common stockholders. In other words, it pays to be a debtor when there is inflation.

(7) Investors and other readers of financial reports cannot make their own inflation adjustments in conventional financial reports. Managements and

outside auditors are the only ones who can prepare and attest such information.

Experiments by Individual Corporations

One outcome of the American Accounting Association's research project was that, during the late 1950's and early 1960's, a small handful of companies actually experimented with the disclosure of inflation-adjusted financial information. But, except in the case of the Reece Corporation (described later), these companies did not follow very closely the recommendations of the AAA's Committee on Concepts and Standards Underlying Corporate Financial Statements. A Conference Board report released in 1962 presented case studies of seven U.S. corporations and one Canadian firm that disclosed various types of inflation-adjusted financial information in their reports to stockholders.[3] For the most part, these firms adjusted their historical-cost depreciation calculations in accordance with a price index; or, in the case of the Canadian corporation, a new depreciation figure was based on the estimated current values of fixed assets. Other financial statement items were not adjusted.

The principal objective of all of these companies was to explain that net incomes reported in accordance with conventional accounting rules were not really as great as they appeared to be. Nevertheless, income taxes were levied on the basis of conventionally determined revenues and expenses. Furthermore, three of the organizations were public utilities whose managements sought to demonstrate that their allowed rates of return were not realistic when based upon conventional accounting rules.

One of the companies whose experiences were described in the 1962 Conference Board report was The Reece Corporation of Waltham, Massachusetts. It had been one of the

[3]Francis J. Walsh, Jr., *Inflation and Corporate Accounting*. National Industrial Conference Board, Studies in Business Policy, No. 104, 1962.

participants in the American Accounting Association's research project.

Because this firm adopted a somewhat different approach to its computation of adjusted net income, the Reece Corporation received quite a lot of attention from researchers who were studying the problems of inflation in accounting at that time. It did not stop with merely recomputing depreciation but, rather, restated all of its account balances in what it called "uniform dollars," or units of purchasing power as of the latest year-end. It set up a system of worksheets in which it applied the Bureau of Labor Statistics Consumer Price Index to every general ledger account balance. These account balances had been analyzed by years of acquisition or incurrence of the items making up the balances.

The restated balances in terms of uniform dollars, when compared with the balances derived by the company's conventional accounting methods, revealed the effects of inflation on the company's income for the year. These comparative figures then formed the basis for some charts and a narrative explanation of the effects of inflation that appeared in the company's annual reports to stockholders. The exhibit on pages 30 and 32 shows the information about inflationary effects that was reported to investors in The Reece Corporation's annual report for 1960.

Another company whose financial statements aroused the interest of accounting researchers two decades ago was N.V. Philips' Gloeilampenfabrieken. Although headquartered in Eindhoven, The Netherlands, this large manufacturing company operates in many countries and is well known to U.S. investors. It was interesting to U.S. accountants because of its restatement of fixed assets in terms of current replacement value, and also because of its recognition of holding gains and losses on monetary items. Following a practice that was approved by The Netherlands business community, the company virtually abandoned the historical-cost principle of accounting and continually adjusted its accounting records so that its nonmonetary assets were restated in terms of current replacement values. Changes in replacement value were charged directly to asset accounts, with the offsetting credits being made to a revaluation surplus account in the "Capital" (or shareholders' equity) section of the balance sheet. Depreciation of property, machinery and equipment was computed directly on the basis of the replacement value balances. In the case of monetary assets, the company used a cost-of-living index to calculate the loss in purchasing power for the period. This loss was charged to an expense account, "Cost of Inflation," and credited to a shareholders' equity account, "Reserve for Diminishing Purchasing Power of Capital Invested in Monetary Assets."[4]

Activities of the American Institute of CPA's

The American Institute of Certified Public Accountants is the national professional society of the public accounting profession. Heavily involved in the establishment of accounting rules since the 1930's, it has a strong interest in the problem of reporting the effects of inflation.[5] As part of its support for the Accounting Principles Board, which came into being in 1959, the Institute greatly expanded its research program. One of the principal projects assigned to this research activity was to study the methods of measuring and reporting inflationary effects on the financial statements of businesss enterprises.

[4]A detailed explanation of the procedures followed by N.V. Philips' Gloeilampenfabrieken appeared in an article by A. Goudeket, "An Application of Replacement Value Theory," *The Journal of Accountancy,* July, 1960.

[5]Francis J. Walsh, Jr., *Identifying Accounting Principles: The Process of Developing Financial Reporting Standards and Rules in the United States.* The Conference Board, Report No. 762, 1979.

Exhibit 1: Portion of Annual Report of The Reece Corporation, 1960, showing effects of inflation on Income

Price Level Study

Although the accompanying audited statements are on a consolidated basis, we are continuing the Price Level Study for The Reece Corporation alone because it is impractical to attempt the necessary adjustments of our subsidiary companies' figures in order to report the Price Level Study on a consolidated basis.

In this Study, the Company's financial statements have been converted, by means of index numbers based on the Consumer's Price Index, from Historical Dollars (those used in conventional accounting and in our reported figures) to Uniform Dollars (defined as uniform measuring units whose purchasing power is equal to 1960 dollars) so that the Company's figures as reported may be compared with statements prepared on a uniform basis.

1960 was another year of relative price stability during which the Consumer's Price Index only rose 1.6%, but continued relatively small increases in this index accumulate rapidly as is demonstrated by the fact that the cost of living has increased 12% during the past 8 years and 24% during the past 12 years. The damaging effects of sharp rises in the cost of living are self-evident, but the consequences of less dramatic increases are not readily apparent without a study such as this.

The accompanying charts compare, on a percentage basis, changes in gross and net income in Historical Dollars and Uniform Dollars. It is well to note that although 1960 gross income expressed in Historical Dollars is more than double that of 1943, in Uniform Dollars (those of a constant purchasing power) the increase is only 34%. The Company's net income before taxes in Historical Dollars is about twice that of 1943, whereas in true purchasing power it increased 27%.

The Reece Corporation (unconsolidated) shows net profit of $1,002,000 for 1960; but after adjustments for price level changes net profit expressed in 1960 Uniform Dollars is $906,000. This

The result of this project was a lengthy research document, "Reporting the Financial Effects of Price-Level Changes," Accounting Research Study No. 6 by the staff of AICPA's Accounting Research Division. This report was published in difference of $96,000 provides for $63,000 additional depreciation and $33,000 additional cost of sales to adjust inventories for the increase in the price level.

Even in a year of relative price stability we find a substantial difference between reported profit, on which income taxes are based, and profit adjusted for price level changes which, in effect, is profit after taking into account the loss of purchasing power of funds invested in fixed assets and inventory. It follows that for 1960 the Federal income tax of about $50,000 applicable to the $96,000 necessary to adjust depreciation and inventories is a capital levy, not an income tax.

Extending this example a bit further, it is not hard to imagine a company which reports a low margin of profit in an inflationary period, but which actually suffers a loss after making adjustments for price level changes, being required to pay so-called income taxes.

This Company's relatively heavy investment in inventory and fixed assets, including machines leased to customers, requires constant awareness of the effects of price level changes. In periods of inflation, a large share of reported earnings must be reinvested in the business to overcome erosion of capital and provide for reasonable growth. This thought is best illustrated by the fact that during the last ten years the book value of the Company's fixed assets has increased 22% in Historical Dollars but only 2% in Uniform Dollars.

W.D. Brooks, Jr., Treasurer

Source: The Reece Corporation, Annual Report, 1960.

1963 and it was the most comprehensive treatment of the subject until that time. The researchers at the AICPA limited the scope of the study to price-level adjustments, that is, adjustments of historical dollar-account balances by the use

Exhibit 1 continued

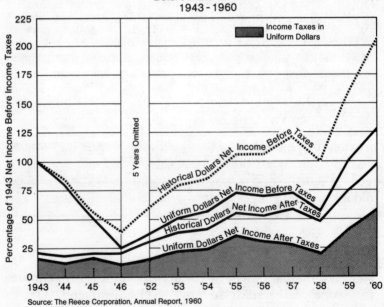

Gross Income
1943 - 1960

Percentage of 1943

5 Years Omitted

Historical Dollars

Uniform Dollars

Net Income
Before and After Taxes
1943 - 1960

Percentage of 1943 Net Income Before Income Taxes

Income Taxes in
Uniform Dollars

5 Years Omitted

Historical Dollars Net Income Before Taxes

Uniform Dollars Net Income Before Taxes

Historical Dollars Net Income After Taxes

Uniform Dollars Net Income After Taxes

Source: The Reece Corporation, Annual Report, 1960

32

of index numbers. They specifically excluded consideration of the use of replacement costs or any approach having to do with current costs.

The Accounting Principles Board of the AICPA deliberated over the implications of Accounting Research Study No. 6 for several years, but finally decided not to issue an opinion which would be mandatory for reporting corporations. Instead, it issued a "Statement." Statements were pronouncements of the APB that did not have the authority of Opinions but were issued primarily for educational or discussion purposes.

The APB Statement on inflation accounting was No. 3, "Financial Statements Restated For General Price Level Changes," issued in June, 1969.[6] Like the AICPA research study that preceded it, the Statement dealt only with what the Board called "general price-level financial statements," that is, financial reports whose historical dollar amounts were restated in terms of present-day dollars by the application of an index of general purchasing-power changes. It did not consider inflation adjustments related to appraisal values, replacement costs, or any other measure of current values.

The Statement sought to (1) explain the effects of changes in the general purchasing power of money; (2) describe the basic nature of financial statements restated for general price-level changes; and (3) give general guidance on how to prepare and present these financial statements.

The Statement emphasized that the effect of changes in the price level on an individual company could not be approximated by a simple adjustment, such as merely recalculating fixed assets and depreciation. Rather, it recommended that a comprehensive restatement of the items making up the financial statements would be needed. The

---

[6]APB Statement No. 3, "Financial Statements Restated for General Price Level Changes," June, 1969. American Institute of Certified Public Accountants, 1211 Avenue of the Americas, New York, New York 10036.

GNP deflator was the index that was favored for the purpose of making such restatements. General purchasing power of the dollar, as of the latest balance sheet date, was the standard for presentation.

An important feature of the Statement was its recognition of so-called "holding gains and losses" on monetary items (described in Chapter 2, p. 4). Such losses and gains, of course, cannot be measured in historical-cost financial statements. But the APB recommended that holding gains and losses be calculated and reported in the comprehensively restated financial reports. An appendix to APB Statement No. 3 contained a lengthy listing of financial statement items classified as to their monetary or nonmonetary characteristics. Another appendix described and illustrated the general procedures, worksheet techniques, and forms of restated financial reports for general price-level financial statements.

The APB concluded that the information derived from these restatements was useful and it recommended (but did not require) that this information be disclosed to the readers of financial statements. It emphasized that such restated financial information should not displace the conventional, historical-cost statements as the basic reports of the enterprise but, rather, it should be presented as a supplementary disclosure.

However, since it was not mandatory, very few companies complied with the APB's recommendations.

SEC Accounting Series Release No. 190

Under the federal securities laws of the 1930's, the Securities and Exchange Commission (SEC) has the power to impose accounting standards and rules on companies that are subject to its jurisdiction. For the most part, the Commission has left accounting rule making in the hands of private-sector agencies such as the AICPA and, later, the FASB. Occasionally, however, the SEC has acted to impose accounting rules of its own. One recent instance of such direct action by the SEC was Accounting Series Release (ASR) No. 190, issued in March, 1976.[7]

This ruling required certain companies registered with the Commission to disclose the estimated current replacement costs of their inventories and fixed assets at the end of each year for which a balance sheet was required. And it mandated the estimation of cost of sales and depreciation expense based on replacement cost for the two most recent full fiscal years. This information was to be presented in the form of footnotes to the conventional, historical cost-based financial statements required under SEC Regulation S-X. Only large corporations were immediately affected by ASR No. 190, since only those registrants having inventories and fixed assets aggregating more than $100 million—that comprised more than 10 percent of their total assets—were bound by the ruling.

The SEC rule was in sharp contrast with the earlier recommendations of the Accounting Principles Board in that it chose replacement cost as the approach to measuring the effect of inflation rather than general price-level adjustments. The SEC also limited its ruling to inventories, fixed assets, cost of sales, and depreciation, while the APB favored comprehensive restatement of all financial statement items. The APB's approach, consequently, permitted a restated net income amount to be identified while the SEC's method did not.

The SEC's ruling was not enthusiastically received. For example, a research study conducted by the Financial Executives Research Foundation indicated that management respondents to its survey overwhelmingly opposed replacement cost disclosure. And most investment analysts

[7]Securities and Exchange Commission, Accounting Series Release No. 190, "Notice of Adoption of Amendments to Regulation S-X Requiring Disclosure of Certain Replacement Cost Data." Washington, D.C. 20549, March 23, 1976.

who were queried did not believe the disclosures required by the SEC were useful in making investment and credit decisions.[8]

Nevertheless, replacement-cost information continued to be required in the filings of affected corporations with the Commission. Finally, in November, 1979, the SEC announced that it had repealed the provisions of ASR No. 190 once the requirements of the FASB became fully effective. As described in an earlier chapter, the FASB released its Statement No. 33, "Financial Reporting and Changing Prices," in October, 1979. Some parts of the FASB's ruling applied to 1979 annual corporate reports and other parts were to become effective in 1980.

The Long Road to Inflation Accounting

This chapter has attempted to summarize the major efforts, over a period of several decades, to arrive at a satisfactory way to report the effects of inflation in the financial statements of business enterprises. Due to limitations of space and the intended scope of this report, only the high spots could be described. Many researchers in professional societies, accounting firms, and universities have contributed to the evolution of thought in this difficult field of accounting. It is not practical to list all of the contributions to the development of inflation accounting, or to describe all of the experiments that have been conducted, because they simply are too numerous.

---

[8]J.W. Frank, T.F. Kealey, and G.W. Silverman, "The Effects and Usefulness of Replacement Cost Disclosure," Financial Executives Research Foundation, 633 Third Avenue, New York, New York 10017, 1978.

Chapter 6
Evaluation of Inflation Accounting

Despite the promulgation of the FASB's new rules, and in spite of the years of study and experimentation that have been spent on inflation accounting, the desirability of publishing inflation-adjusted financial reports still is far from a settled issue in the minds of many people.

Opposition to Inflation Accounting

Opponents of inflation accounting declare that attempts to adjust the financial reports of business enterprises so that the distortive effects of changing prices are minimized is so complex and so confusing that the effort is simply not worthwhile. They point out that the reader of a shareholders' report containing the information mandated by the FASB in 1979 has not just one—but a choice among *three different amounts*—as the firm's "true" net income, earnings per share, and shareholders' equity. These three alternatives are: (1) the conventional historical cost-based computation (sometimes labeled "as reported in the principal financial statements"); (2) computations in terms of "constant dollars," and (3) amounts based on "current costs." If investors find conventional annual reports confusing, the critics ask, how much worse will be their plight when confronted with the bewildering array of inflation-adjusted data?

Corporate managements, too, have generally been unenthusiastic about inflation-adjusted financial reporting. The principal reason is that the application of this accounting refinement usually results in a reduction of a firm's reported net income below that which is determined by conventional historical-cost methods. Not only does this reduction make management look bad, but it could impair the amounts available for incentive-compensation purposes.

Other opponents of inflation accounting protest that the objectivity of financial reporting is undermined when any basis other than conventional historical cost is introduced into the measurement process. They object most strenuously to the use of current-cost accounting because, by its nature, it requires the repeated restatement of major financial statement components, such as fixed assets and depreciation. These critics feel that such restatements are based on essentially subjective judgments and that the verifiable benchmark of historical cost is cast aside. They believe that abandonment of the historical-cost basis seriously reduces the credibility and verifiability of financial reporting. They also object to restatements in terms of constant dollars, although not so strenuously, because that measurement approach is at least tied to historical cost. But they still feel that it is a dangerous compromise that impairs the integrity of accounting.

Still another school of thought opposes inflation accounting on the grounds of monetary philosophy. Those who hope for the return of sound money believe that giving accounting recognition to changes in prices amounts to a final concession that the dollar is, in fact, unstable. Critics who object to inflation adjustments on these grounds argue that inflation accounting aids the forces who, they believe, are leading the nation down the primrose path to the ultimate collapse of the dollar and financial ruin.

Arguments in Favor of Inflation Accounting

Supporters of the idea of inflation-adjusted financial reports base their arguments essentially on the principle of economic realism. They believe that the experience of recent years clearly demonstrates the instability of the dollar. Furthermore, they have little confidence that the nation's political leaders and economic policymakers have either the ability or the will to stem the forces of severe inflation. Consequently, they feel that accounting must adapt to these real-world conditions—to report the facts as they are—if accounting is to retain its usefulness as an aid to decision making.

Another manifestation of the realism principle is the argument that, to combat inflation, the national economy desperately needs to improve its productivity, and that the way to improve productivity is to stimulate capital investment. Supporters of inflation accounting believe that an important incentive to invest in new, improved production facilities would come from reform of the existing depreciation provisions of the federal income tax laws. They argue that the business community needs to demonstrate that it sincerely believes capital is being eroded by inadequate depreciation allowances. Business, according to this view, can show its sincerity by reporting depreciation expense to investors based on inflation-adjusted data. The business community cannot claim much credibility in Congress when it asks for more generous tax depreciation allowances while at the same time reporting high earnings, based on historical-cost depreciation to investors. In short, business will never be able to escape the onus of so-called "obscene profits" until it acknowledges that historical cost-based profits are illusory and emphasizes instead the realities of inflation-adjusted earnings.

A related argument in favor of inflation adjustments is that boards of directors and shareholders both need to be informed of the distortive effects of inflation on the reported net incomes of their corporations. Historical cost-based net income is usually exaggerated, principally because depreciation expense is understated. These inflated earnings create demands from investors for dividend increases that boards of directors find hard to resist. Reporting lower net incomes as a result of applying inflation adjustments would help to relieve such pressures and would have the desirable effect of preserving corporate capital, in the opinion of those who favor inflation-adjusted financial reporting. They add that it is unreasonable to expect investors, or any other readers of corporate financial reports, to make their own allowances for inflationary distortions. Inflation does not affect all companies equally and only management, aided by outside auditors, is in a position to make such measurements.

In answer to the objection that inflation adjustments undermine the integrity of accounting by moving away from the firm, objectively verifiable base of historical costs, supporters of the new techniques point out that constant-dollar accounting in no way abandons historical cost. It simply restates historical dollars in terms of their current purchasing power through the application of a price index. Even current-cost adjustments are made in accordance with procedures that are verifiable—such as the application of externally developed price indexes for the class of goods being measured, or determination of direct prices from current vendors' invoices or quotations. Also, defenders of inflation adjustments point out that recommendations of accounting standard-setting agencies have always emphasized that historical-cost financial statements are the *primary* reports of any enterprise; inflation-adjusted data are always to be presented as *supplementary* information. The historical-cost reports are always there for anyone who wants them.

Generally, proponents of inflation accounting techniques are not so enthusiastic that they give it unrestrained support. They acknowledge that the best thing to do about inflation is to adopt the economic and political measures that are needed to stop it. All that accounting can do is to provide some indication of what inflation does to individual companies and to provide managers and investors with tools for decision making in an inflationary environment. They recognize, too, that existing methodologies for measuring the impact of changing prices on business leave something to be desired. Nevertheless, they feel that it is better to give the best information that is available—even though it is admittedly imperfect—rather than ignore the problem altogether.

Further Study Needed

At the present time, only a relatively small number of the largest corporations are affected by the FASB's ruling on "Financial Reporting and Changing Prices." The vast majority of business enterprises have yet to face the problem. And the FASB has repeatedly stressed the need for experimentation and study to develop better ways of measuring and reporting the effects of changing prices. It has also declared its intention to monitor closely the experience of companies and investors with inflation-adjusted information. The Board is particularly interested in the effects of its statement on the behavior of investors and of corporate managements.

Practically all of the attention that has been focused on inflation accounting during the last two decades has concentrated on external financial reporting. Very little study has been given to the application of these techniques to internal management-reporting systems. Perhaps one reason for this apparent neglect is the assumption that well-informed managers intuitively take inflation into account during the decision-making process, whether or not explicit information is given to them. However that may be, some financial executives are concerned that bad pricing decisions and erroneous return-on-investment computations are resulting from the failure to supply some inflationary measurements to internal decision makers. The approaches to, and methods for, doing this have yet to be worked out.

Appendix

Summary of FASB Statement No. 33

Appendix

STATEMENT OF
FINANCIAL ACCOUNTING STANDARDS No. 33*

Financial Reporting and Changing Prices

SUMMARY

This Statement applies to public enterprises that have either (1) inventories and property, plant, and equipment (before deducting accumulated depreciation) amounting to more than $125 million or (2) total assets amounting to more than $1 billion (after deducting accumulated depreciation).

No changes are to be made in the primary financial statements; the information required by the Statement is to be presented as supplementary information in published annual reports.

For fiscal years ended on or after December 25, 1979, enterprises are required to report:

a. Income from continuing operations adjusted for the effects of general inflation

b. The purchasing power gain or loss on net monetary items.

For fiscal years ended on or after December 25, 1979, enterprises are also required to report:

a. Income from continuing operations on a current cost basis

b. The current cost amounts of inventory and property, plant, and equipment at the end of the fiscal year

c. inventory and property, plant, and equipment, net of inflation.

However, information on a current cost basis for fiscal years ended before December 25, 1980 may be presented in the first annual report for a fiscal year ended on or after December 25, 1980.

Enterprises are required to present a five-year summary of selected financial data, including information on income, sales and other operating revenues, net assets, dividends per common share, and market price per share. In the computation of net assets, only inventory and property, plant, and equipment need to be adjusted for the effects of changing prices.

Illustrative formats for disclosure of the required information are included in this Summary as Schedules A, B, and C (pages 32-34 of the Statement).

To present the supplementary information required by this Statement, an enterprise needs to measure the effects of changing prices on inventory, property, plant, and equipment, cost of goods sold, and depreciation, depletion, and amortization expense. No adjustments are required to other revenues, expenses, gains, and losses.

In computations of current cost income, expenses are to be measured at current cost or lower recoverable amount. Current cost measures relate to the assets owned and used by the enterprise and not to other assets that might be acquired to replace the assets owned. This Statement allows considerable flexibility in choice of sources of information about current costs: An enterprise may use specific price indexes or other evidence of a more direct nature. This Statement also encourages simplifications in computations and other aspects of implementation: In particular, "recoverable amounts" need be measured only if they are judged to be significantly and permanently lower than current cost; that situation is unlikely to occur very often.

The Board believes that this Statement meets an urgent need for information about the effects of changing prices. If that information is not provided: Resources may be allocated inefficiently; investors' and creditors' understanding of the past performance of an enterprise and their ability to assess future cash flows may be severely limited; and people in government who participate in decisions on economic policy may lack important information about the implication of their decisions. The requirements of the Statement are expected to promote a better understanding by the general public of the problems caused by inflation: Statements by business managers about those problems are unlikely to have sufficient credibility until financial reports provide quantitative information about the effects of inflation.

Special problems arise in the application of the current cost requirements of this Statement to certain types of assets, notably natural resources and income-producing real estate property. The Board will consider those problems further and address them in an Exposure Draft with a view to publishing a Statement in 1980. This Statement gives guidance on the treatment of those assets and related expenses for enterprises that present current cost information for fiscal years ending before December 25, 1980.

This Statement calls for two supplementary income computations, one dealing with the effects of changes in the prices of resources used by the enterprise. The Board believes that both types of information are likely to be useful. Comment letters on the Exposure Draft revealed differences of opinion on the relative usefulness of the two approaches. Many preparers and public accounting firms emphasized the need to deal with the effects of general inflation; users generally preferred information dealing with the effects of specific price changes. The Board believes that further experimentation is required on the usefulness of the two types of information and that experimentation is possible only if both are provided by large public enterprises. The Board intends to assess the usefulness of the information called for by this Statement. That assessment will provide a basis for ongoing decisions on whether or not provision of both types of information should be continued and on whether other requirements in this Statement should be reviewed. The Board will undertake a comprehensive review of this Statement no later than five years after its publication.

The measurement and use of information on changing prices will require a substantial learning process on the part of all concerned. In view of the importance of clear explanations to users of financial reports of the significance of the information, the Board is organizing an advisory group to develop and publish illustrative disclosures that might be appropriate as a guide to preparers in particular industries.

SCHEDULE A

STATEMENT OF INCOME FROM CONTINUING OPERATIONS ADJUSTED FOR CHANGING PRICES
For the Year Ended December 31, 1980

(In 000s of Average 1980 Dollars)

Income from continuing operations, as reported in the income statement		$ 9,000
Adjustments to restate costs for the effect of general inflation		
Cost of goods sold	(7,384)	
Depreciation and amortization expense	(4,130)	(11,514)
Loss from continuing operations adjusted for general inflation		(2,514)
Adjustments to reflect the difference between general inflation and changes in specific prices (current costs)		
Cost of goods sold	(1,024)	
Depreciation and amortization expense	(5,370)	(6,394)
Loss from continuing operations adjusted for changes in specific prices		$(8,908)
Gain from decline in purchasing power of net amounts owed		$ 7,729
Increase in specific prices (current cost) of inventories and property, plant, and equipment held during the year*		$ 24,608
Effect of increase in general price level		18,959
Excess of increase in specific prices over increase in the general price level		$ 5,649

---

* At December 31, 1980 current cost of inventory was $65,700 and current cost of property, plant, and equipment, net of accumulated depreciation was $85,100.

STATEMENT OF INCOME FROM CONTINUING OPERATIONS ADJUSTED FOR CHANGING PRICES
For the Year Ended December 31, 1980

(In 000s of Dollars)

	As Reported in the Primary Statements	Adjusted for General Inflation	Adjusted for Changes in Specific Prices (Current Costs)
Net sales and other operating revenues	$253,000	$253,000	$253,000
Cost of goods sold	197,000	204,384	205,408
Depreciation and amortization expense	10,000	14,130	19,500
Other operating expense	20,835	20,835	20,835
Interest expense	7,165	7,165	7,165
Provision for income taxes	9,000	9,000	9,000
	244,000	255,514	261,908
Income (loss) from continuing operations	$ 9,000	$(2,514)	$(8,908)
Gain from decline in purchasing power of net amounts owed		$ 7,729	$ 7,729
Increase in specific prices (current cost) of inventories and property, plant, and equipment held during the year*			$ 24,608
Effect of increase in general price level			18,959
Excess of increase in specific prices over increase in the general price level			$ 5,649

*At December 31, 1980 current cost of inventory was $65,700 and current cost of property, plant, and equipment, net of accumulated depreciation was $85,100.

SCHEDULE C

FIVE-YEAR COMPARISON OF SELECTED
SUPPLEMENTARY FINANCIAL DATA ADJUSTED FOR EFFECTS OF CHANGING PRICES

(In 000s of Average 1980 Dollars)

	Years Ended December 31,				
	1976	1977	1978	1979	1980
Net sales and other operating revenues	265,000	235,000	240,000	237,063	253,000
Historical cost information adjusted for general inflation					
Income (loss) from continuing operations				(2,761)	(2,514)
Income (loss) from continuing operations per common share				$ (1.91)	$ (1.68)
Net assets at year-end				55,518	57,733
Current cost information					
Income (loss) from continuing operations				(4,125)	(8,908)
Income (loss) from continuing operations per common share				$ (2.75)	$ (5.94)
Excess of increase in specific prices over increase in the general price level				2,292	5,649
Net assets at year-end				79,996	81,466
Gain from decline in purchasing power of net amounts owed				7,027	7,729
Cash dividends declared per common share	$ 2.59	$ 2.43	$ 2.26	$ 2.16	$ 2.00
Market price per common share at year-end	$ 32	$ 31	$ 43	$ 39	$ 35
Average consumer price index	170.5	181.5	195.4	205.0	220.9